Tithing & Stewardship: Kingdom Money Matters

Frederick O. Towles

ISBN: 978-0-692-51367-5

DEDICATION

This book is dedicated to all those who desire to tithe but haven't because of lack of faith, incorrect teaching or who simply didn't know.

This book is also dedicated to leaders in the community of faith who have stayed in the fight despite the obstacles they face.

HOPE - FAITH - ESPERAR-HOPE - FAITH - ESPERAR-HOPE - FAITH - ESPERAR-HOPE - FAITH - ESPERAR - HOPE - FAITH

UE

UNLIMITED EXPECTATIONS

ACKNOWLEDGMENTS

I'd like to acknowledge my wife, family, mentors, business associates and colleagues. Each of you have contributed something to my life that has made me better.

Tithing and Stewardship

This writing is geared, in general, to address the topic of tithing, but more specifically, is an attempt to raise your understanding of stewardship. In order to do this, we must first speak about tithing and where it began:

The Tithe

Tithing is a Biblical principle instituted before the Law of Moses. Tithing means a tenth – 10% of one's increase – what you have earned or have been given. In fact, tithing is the first level of financial stewardship. This is what the Bible is speaking of in Malachi 3:10-12:

"*Bring the whole tithe into the storehouse, that there may be food in my house. Test me in this, says the Lord Almighty, and see if I will not throw open the floodgates of Heaven and pour out so much blessing that there will not be room enough to store it. I will prevent pests from devouring your crops, and the vines in your field will not drop their fruit before it is ripe, says the Lord Almighty. Then all nations will call you blessed, for yours will be a delightful land, says the Lord Almighty.*"

The children of Israel were bringing what they thought the Lord considered a tithe, but they fell short. What does that mean? They were bringing less than a tenth and considering that amount – less than ten percent – and counting that as a tithe. That is why the children of Israel were considered thieves, because they were robbing God from the amount of their increase they were required to bring.

I can hear the New Testament theologians saying, "Tithing is an Old Testament principle." That can be a debate or discussion we can have at a later time. But for the New Testament theologians, think about this -- What is the difference in Old Testament Israel not bringing the entire tithe and the Acts Chapter 5 financial impropriety of Ananias and his wife Sapphira? In both situations, falsehood was exhibited. Definitely something to ponder.

As stated earlier, the tithe is the first phase of financial stewardship. It sets the tone for your financial journey. In most personal development books I have read, the element of tithing is seen. Many personal development books suggest that the rich give ten percent of their earnings to a non-profit organization, or to assist other people. Isn't that interesting? There is something about giving away the tenth of your increase that causes things to happen that wouldn't necessarily occur under normal conditions.

The Bible, in Malachi 3, describes this "occurrence" vividly. God says, "*I will throw open the floodgates of Heaven and pour out so much blessing that there won't be room to store it.*" This means that God will prevent you from experiencing lack. He didn't say you would be rich, although you could be, but the emphasis here is – lack will depart from your life.

God's promises continue with a promise of protection. Israel was a culture heavily dependent on agriculture and marine life -- growing crops and fishing. God promised to protect their assets and their ability to produce from the threat of outside predators – "*I will prevent pests from devouring your crops.*" What can compare to the promises of God? There are many strategies on the market to protect one's assets, but none can protect them like God can.

The third layer of God's promises to someone who brings the entire tithe is perfect timing. He says, "*The vines in your field will not drop their fruit before it is ripe.*" In business, timing can be the difference between being successful or unsuccessful. If you bring a product or service to the market too soon, even if people need it -- if the timing is not right -- it may not be welcomed. If you bring a product or service to the market too late, you will have to fight a plethora of competitors. But if you come to the market at just the right time, you can find huge success. It is the same principle with timing and the tithe. God's Word does not lie. Whatever it says, that is what will happen.

The fourth layer of God's promises to the tither is

having people take notice of what is happening with you. God desires His children to succeed and when they obey His Word, He will always spotlight them. God tells Israel, again in Malachi 3, "*Then all nations will call you blessed, for yours will be a delightful land, says the Lord Almighty.*"

What an awesome plan, and it only costs us obedience to God's word and 10% of our income!

The 90%

The second phase of financial stewardship is managing the remaining ninety percent. This is where many people don't do well. I would like to speak to this topic from a Biblical perspective.

First, let's define what *stewardship* is. The Merriam Webster Dictionary defines *stewardship* as the conducting, supervising, or managing of something; especially the careful and responsible management of something entrusted to one's care.

Second, we must remember that: (1) everything belongs to the Lord; He is the owner and (2) He has allowed us the privilege and has entrusted us to manage the resources He has given.

In a similar way, if you are a parent, God has entrusted you with the responsibility to raise -- carefully manage and supervise -- your children. And, if you have a position of leadership in any other area, this principle works the same way.

When it comes to finances, we are to be good stewards over what has been entrusted to us, no matter how small or how large the amount may seem. Let's take a look at an example of stewardship in the Bible -- the parable of the talents in Matthew 25:14-30:

"Again, it will be like a man going on a journey, who called his servants and entrusted his wealth to them. To one he gave five bags of gold, to another two bags, and to another one bag, each according to his ability. Then he went on his journey. The man who had received five bags of gold went at once and put his money to work and gained five bags more. So also, the one with two bags of gold gained two more. But the man who had received one bag went off, dug a hole in the ground and hid his master's money. After a long time, the master of those servants returned and settled accounts with them. The man who had received five bags of gold

brought the other five. 'Master, he said, You entrusted me with five bags of gold. See, I have gained five more.' His master replied, 'Well done, good and faithful servant! You have been faithful with a few things; I will put you in charge of many things. Come and share your Master's happiness!' The man with two bags of gold also came. 'Master, he said, You entrusted me with two bags of gold; see, I have gained two more.' His master replied, 'Well done, good and faithful servant! You have been faithful with a few things; I will put you in charge of many things. Come and share your master's happiness!' Then the man who had received one bag of gold came. 'Master, he said, I knew that you were a hard man, harvesting where you have not sown and gathering where you have not scattered seed. So I was afraid and went out and hid your gold in the ground. See, here is what belongs to you.' His master replied, 'You wicked, lazy servant!' So you knew that I harvest where I have not sown and gather where I have not scattered seed? Well then, you should have put my money on deposit with the bankers, so that when I returned I would have received it back with interest. So take the bag of gold from him and give it to the one who has ten bags. For whoever has, will be given more, and they will have an abundance. Whoever does not have, even what they have will be taken from them. And throw that worthless servant outside, into the darkness, where there will be weeping and gnashing of teeth."

In this periscope – an extract from a text (in this

case the Biblical text), each of the three servants were entrusted with a certain amount of the owner's wealth. Keep in mind that each talent or bag of gold was equivalent to 20 years of a person's wages. What were these servants supposed to do with the funds that were entrusted to them? Save, spend, or manage them? There were no instructions given in the Biblical text, so how would one know?

The first two servants managed the funds they were entrusted with and doubled the amount they received. The last servant's encounter shows us the heart of the Master. The Master wanted the servants to manage the money they received. In other words, the Master wanted the servants to be good financial stewards over the funds given to them. God's desire is for us to be responsible stewards of the ninety percent. This means we have to learn to manage our resources well – particularly money, but not only limited to money.

How do we manage our resources well? First, let's define what it means to *manage*. The dictionary defines *manage* as having control of something such as a business, department, team, etc., or to take care of and make decisions about someone's time, money, etc. God has given us the ability to make decisions and to have control over the ninety percent. There are a number of ways we can do this, each of which is described previously in the Matthew 25 text:

Know the heart and desire of the Master: The third servant knew that the Master would return and upon his return He would seek to find out what was done with the funds entrusted to him. There were no instructions needed at the time that the bag of gold was given to the third servant. There was already an understanding by the third servant that the Master would seek a gain on what was originally disbursed. Likewise, you and I must understand what God is looking for us to do with the resources we have been given. This information comes to us through prayer, teaching, and the reading of God's word as it pertains to managing our resources of time, talent, and money.

<u>Don't waste effort</u>: The third servant knowing his Master's desire, took action, but took the incorrect action. Many people are in the Kingdom generating tremendous action. The question is: Are they conducting the correct action? Incorrect action wastes time. Wasted effort equals wasted energy, ultimately resulting in wasted time. Let's make every effort count. Time, being our most precious commodity, should never be wasted.

<u>Invest wisely</u>: Because the Master is seeking a return on what has been entrusted to us, it is important that we invest wisely. Investing wisely speaks to areas such as our time, talents and finances. We must invest wisely in order to produce a return, which the Master expects upon His return.

<u>Be diligent</u>: Being diligent means to consistently take the proper action, even when you don't feel like it. I have read many books and heard even more stories. It is rare to hear a success story that doesn't include consistent proper action. Therefore, we must be diligent about the way we manage what has been entrusted to us.

Posture

When we are discussing stewardship, posture – the approach or attitude to giving - must be addressed. Billy Graham once said, "A checkbook is a theological document; it will tell you who and what you worship." Pastor Rick Warren also addressed this issue by once saying, "Show me your schedule and your checkbook stubs and, no matter what you say is important, I'll tell you what's really important to you."

What we must understand is tithing and stewardship is just as much a spiritual discipline as prayer. Giving shows where our heart is towards God. Matthew 6:21 says, "for where your treasure is, there your heart will be also." So the first part of our posture in tithing and stewardship is that we must prioritize what we spend and where we spend our resources. Based on the Matthew 6 verse, wherever our affection lies our resource (money, time and talent) will follow. Where is the majority of your resources diverted to?

The second part of posture in giving and stewardship is our approach. According to 2 Corinthians 9:6-7:

"Remember this: whoever sows sparingly will also reap sparingly, and whoever sows generously will also reap generously. Each of you should give what you have decided in your heart to give, not reluctantly or under compulsion, for God loves a cheerful giver."

Paul alerts the members of the church at Corinth that they should give to the ministry willingly. He didn't want the people to give under any conditions of pressure or to be tricked into giving. This is why Paul encourages the people to give what was purposed in their heart to give with the understanding that if they sowed (gave) sparingly that they would reap sparingly.

Believers should not be pressured, theologically tricked or threatened to give. People should be encouraged to give whatever is in their heart to give. There is a chance that some may not be cheerful when they are giving money, especially if they see it as giving money away. But, leaders should trust the Holy Spirit to move upon the hearts of these people to give generously.

The third part of posture is our outlook on giving. It may appear to an outsider that one is simply giving money away, but in fact we are investing in God's kingdom when we give. Our contributions to the work of the ministry causes the ministry to make progress towards its purpose – to reconcile men and women back to the Father.

In closing, there are several misconceptions and questions about tithing and financial stewardship. Here are some of them:

"As long as I tithe, I will be blessed."

This is a classic misconception about tithing. If you consistently give the complete tithe, you have obeyed God. But this doesn't mean that you should simply do whatever you want with the remaining 90%. Remember, God still requires responsible stewardship. Also, remember that financial stewardship is twofold – tithing and good management over the remaining portion.

"I can't afford to tithe!"

This is another classic misconception. Typically, people who say this fall into one of three categories. The first group understands the principle of tithing but has not been able to adequately manage its finances, resulting in overspending. The second group understands the principle of tithing but has a low level of faith. This group doesn't believe that God is able to do what He promises in the book of Malachi, and throughout the Bible. The last group consists of people who do not understand the principle of tithing, or simply have no desire to tithe.

Isn't tithing an Old Testament concept which represents the Law. If we, the New Testament Church are operating in grace, should we still be tithing?

There are a few things here that we must speak to first. In scripture, tithing is first seen in the Old Testament, Genesis 14:18-20:

"Then Melchizedek King of Salem brought out bread and wine. He was priest of God Most High, and he blessed Abram, saying, "Blessed be Abram by God Most High, Creator of heaven and earth. And blessed be God Most High, who delivered your enemies into your hand." ***Then Abram gave him a tenth of everything****."*

As you can see from the verses above, Abram (Abraham) was never commanded to bring or give the king of Salem a tithe. In fact, the King of Salem came out to Abram to celebrate Abram's victory and to pronounce a blessing upon him.

Second, the first tithe wasn't requested, it was freely given. Abram in honor of Melchizedek (who is a type of Christ) willingly surrendered a tenth of what he had recently received to the King.

Tithing initially was an act of love and honor. When tithing became part of the Law, it became an act of obedience to God. And this is, what makes tithing applicable to the New Testament church, love. When the believer loves and desires to honor God, a tenth isn't an Old Testament or New Testament issue, it is a love issue.

1 John 2: 3-6 says," *We know that we have come to know Him if we obey His commands. The man who says, 'I know Him,' but does not do what He commands is a liar, and the truth is not in him. But if anyone obeys His Word, God's love is truly made complete in him. This is how we know we are in Him.*

Tithing should not be a battle of New Testament or Old Testament, but an issue of a person's heart leaning or being bent towards God. This is not meant to demonize those that don't tithe, but to encourage them to see tithing as an act of love and honor for God. The more we love God, the less things like tithing become an issue.

Here is my last observation about the Old Testament and New Testament conflict about tithing. Read 2 Corinthians 9: 6-15 and Malachi 3:10-12. There are three similarities that both writers are speak to.

First, both Paul (the author of 2 Corinthians) and

Malachi are speaking about the support for the work of God – Malachi from an agricultural resource support and Paul financial.

Second, Paul and Malachi both present the case of God's blessing to those that give, each from slightly different approaches. Malachi speaks of God's blessing on those who tithe while Paul speaks of God blessing to the people and this is the reason to give to the work of the ministry.

Third, both writers agreed that others would look on those that gave with gratefulness – Malachi called them blessed and Paul says, "men will praise God for the obedience that accompanies your confession… and for your generosity."

Where is the money going?

Unfortunately because of bad press, the Church has fallen upon the scrutiny of many of its donors. Because giving overall (tithe and offering) is a love related exchange, as we have established earlier, we must trust that the funds are being managed well. God doesn't hold the tither responsible for how the money given to the church is managed – unless you are one of the people entrusted by God to manage the money of the House. The tither's job is to donate in obedience to God.

Every person will give an account to God for their actions and thoughts. We must trust God that those who He has selected to oversee the assets of the Church are doing what is right. If they are not, God knows and sees what is happening and ultimately, He will handle any wrongdoing.

Should I pay the tithe from my gross or net amount?

This is another one of those questions that has caused many believers to be split in their choice of how much to tithe. The Bible doesn't give any commentary as to gross or net pay because the children of Israel originally dealt in the farming and fishing industries. Therefore calculating a tenth of what they earned was easier.

Now that we have to deal with net and gross pay, the decision is a little different. Here is what I will say, since Social Security, Medicare, Federal, state and local taxes are taken from the gross pay then the tithe should be paid from the gross pay. So that would mean an individual who is paid $39,000.00 per year gross ($750.00 per week) would contribute $75.00 per week for the tithe ($750.00 @ 10%).

A tithe should also be paid from any increase outside of employment. This means that if an individual earns or is given a dollar amount in addition to regular pay then that person would offer a tenth (or tithe) of the newly gained revenue.

I have been tithing consistently, but my financial "ship" hasn't come in yet. What went wrong?

This may not be a question that has been uttered in public, but it has been discussed in closed sessions and pondered in the minds of some. In order to answer this question we must address two areas: teaching and expectation.

Many believers have been taught that when they tithe, God will miraculously give them a twenty, thirty, forty, fifty percent increase or more. That is not proper teaching of what is said in the Scriptures. It sounds good, especially if you are in need of such an increase. But, the Scriptures teach that God will prevent tithers from experiencing lack, have protection from loss, experience perfect timing and people will take notice of them, as mentioned in my earlier points.

Based on the interpretation of tithing benefits and the cunning of some teachers of the Bible, people have been led to believe that God will match His children's contribution dollar for dollar. This is not a 401k, God never promised an exchange of money.

Don't get me wrong, we have all heard that testimony where a tither gets up and says that God blessed them financially. I am not saying that *won't* happen, but I am not saying that it *will* happen, because God is sovereign. Let's remember that the children of Israel, as they were going through the wilderness did not suffer lack either – they were fed from Heaven daily, protected night and day, their clothing and shoes did not wear down – even after a 40-year journey. So every tither may not see an abundance of cash, but they may experience an abundance in provision or good health.

Remember lack means that there is something you don't have enough of. Sometimes the Lord gives us just enough, this is why in addition to tithing, we have to ensure that we manage what we have accurately, because we may get just enough of something.

Where is the window of Heaven blessing for me?

Typically when I hear this question, it refers to a financial return on the tithe that was given. As I stated in the previous question, tithing is not a 401K package – God isn't matching our contribution to His plan dollar for dollar.

Once the person hears that response, they typically reference Luke 6:38:

Give, and it will be given to you. A good measure, pressed down, shaken together and running over, will be poured into your lap. For with the measure you use, it will be measure to you.

Let me be clear. We should not give to God to receive. God cannot be bribed, bought or have His arm twisted. The late Larry Burkett in his book entitled, *Giving And Tithing: Induces Serving And Stewardship*, says the following:

"The spiritual principle behind Luke 6:38 is indeed giving and receiving, but it is not giving to receive. The prerequisites to receiving are found in Luke 6:27-37. A Christian who lives by these principles practices the surrendered life. Therefore, giving is simply a material expression of the deeper spiritual obedience to Christ."

Let's give to God exclusively because we love Him.

I have heard so much about the misuse of money and resources in churches, why should I give?

Our job is to obey God, first and foremost. All the stories we hear about financial misconduct within churches may or may not be true. Nonetheless, we must continue to obey God. There are some that use this as an excuse not to give at all. Don't allow that to be you.

Besides money, what else does stewardship entail?

We should be good stewards in every area of our lives, mainly our time (how we spend our time), talent (how we use our talents) and our treasure (how we manage our resources). I have found in order to be a good steward over any area means you have to plan, be intentional and execute well.

Being intentional means that your mindset has to be shifted in the areas of your life that you want to manage better. This may call for the reading of books about managing those areas, speaking to a trusted group or a professional about helping you to improve.

Whatever it is for you, stewardship takes intentionality – your mind must be made up. As the mindset is being shifted, a plan must be developed to lay out how you will now manage those areas of your life. Once the plan is developed, the next step is to execute the plan.

What portion of my time and talent should I give?

This may be a new or uncomfortable concept to some people. As members of the faith community, it is important that we surrender a portion of our time and talent to serve others.

There are two main reason why we should surrender a portion of our time and talent to serve others::

First, our example, Jesus, was a servant according to Mark 10:45 and Philippians 2:4-7:

"For even the Son of Man came not to be served but to serve, and to give his life as a ransom for many."- Mark 10:45

"Each of you should look not only to your own interests, but also to the interests of others. Your attitude should be the same as that of Christ Jesus; who, being in very nature God, did not consider equality with God something to be grasped, but made himself nothing, taking the very nature of a servant, being made in human likeness" – Philippians 2:4-7

Second, we have been commissioned through the Scriptures to serve others. Galatians 5:13 admonishes us to serve others:

"You, my brothers, were called to be free. But do not use your freedom to indulge the sinful nature; rather, serve one another in love." – Galatians 5:13

Ok, so I get it, I should use my time and talent to serve others, but where do I begin?

If you don't know how much time to begin with, try tithing some of your time and talent to serve others. In a week there is a total of 168 hours, try to carve out sixteen to seventeen hours per week to serve others. This sounds like a lot of time, but in reality, even for the busiest person it isn't, if it is planned correctly.

Service to others should probably be done in an area you like or involving a skill that you like to use. Here are a few examples of things people have done inside and outside the church. Some areas of service could be: cutting the yard of an elderly person in your neighborhood, going to the market for an elderly person and delivering the groceries, volunteering at a hospital or school, teaching Sunday School, ushering, etc. The areas of opportunity are endless and there are so many people who can use assistance.

Once you are engaged in the service of others, you will be surprised how time flies and how rewarding it is to you.

For a more robust financial perspective, refer to my book, *Project Debt Free,* and to a forthcoming book entitled, *Project Debt Free 2.0 For Couples*. Both can be obtained on my website: www.fredericktowles.com.

I pray that this writing helps to clarify the elements of tithing and financial stewardship for you, and that the Lord will continually guide you to a solid understanding of these important Biblical principles.

All verses that appear in this book are quoted from the New International Version (NIV) of the Bible.

Larry Burkett reference comes from his book Giving & Tithing Includes Serving and Stewardship © 1991.

ABOUT THE AUTHOR

Frederick O. Towles is a husband, businessman, public speaker, writer and coach. He enjoys spending time with family, studying, teaching, conducting business and is a sports enthusiast.

Mr. Towles holds a MBA in Business from the University of Phoenix and a Masters of Divinity in Urban Studies from Alliance Theological Seminary.

For more information, other resources or to request Mr. Towles for speaking engagements and coaching please visit www.fredericktowles.com.

Made in the USA
Monee, IL
04 November 2026

67379631R00022